Copyright (c) 2024 by Neils Ribeiro-Yemofio. All rights reserved. No part of this publication may be reproduced, scanned distributed, or transmitted in any form or by any means, including photocopying, recording, or other electronic or mechanical methods, without the prior written permission of the publisher, except in the case of brief quotations embodied in critical reviews and certain other noncommercial uses permitted by copyright law.

Thank you for buying an authorized edition of this book and for complying with copyright laws.

Any resemblance to actual events or persons, living or dead, is entirely coincidental. This is in no form meant for harm nor do we promote harm. Personal perspective use only. Please do not copy/mimic any words or illustration from this book.

Written by Neils Ribeiro-Yemofio.

Manufactured in the United States.

For more books and information, visit us at: www.heroesforhirellc.com and @heroes4hirellc on Instagram.

To Shamelle, Ian, and Jaden. Thank you for making my dreams become reality.

Table of Contents

Introduction

My name is Neils Ribeiro-Yemofio. I am a husband, father, comic-book nerd, and a lover of social impact. Most of my career has been spent in the nonprofit sector, whether it was a national volunteer program, after-school tutoring program, or an anti-poverty program – I've worked there and done everything from recruiting volunteers to securing multi-million dollar donations. I believe in the power of nonprofits and think some leaders and organizations can change the world through operationally being a nonprofit. More importantly, I believe some leaders in the world have an amazing idea, a world-changing idea, a life-saving idea that, through the medium of nonprofits, could exist and do good in the world. All that is holding back these entrepreneurs and these ideas from existing is the knowledge of how to start and run a nonprofit. And that is why I have written **Vision to Reality.**

Since 2017, through my consulting firm, Heroes for Hire, we have helped dreamers, leaders, and social entrepreneurs turn their ideas for change into fully functional nonprofit organizations. Our entrepreneurs have made it to the Forbes list, won national awards, received million-dollar grants, and have made an impact on thousands of lives across the world. After consulting with hundreds of entrepreneurs, I have decided to combine all of the best practices amassed throughout the years into this handbook. Through this handbook you'll learn to:

- Determine if a Nonprofit is Right for You
- Bring Together Your Board of Directors
- Create Your Bylaws
- Understand Conflict Of Interest
- Grasp the Basics of Fundraising
- File Registration Forms

If you purchased this handbook, that means you have an idea for change that has been brewing in your head for some time OR you're curious about how nonprofits work. Either way, you're in the right place.

My approach to this handbook is to simplify the complex, give you a little insight into each of the steps, and give you enough directions to start your nonprofit organization TODAY.

Determine if a Nonprofit is Right for You

If I were to ever talk to you about your idea, or work with you directly, the first question I would ask you is, **"Why does this need to be a nonprofit?"**

Many organizations can do good work, but a nonprofit, and by nonprofit I mean a 501(c)3, is a particular organization used for a particular type of work.

For-Profit

Now, if you just wanted to start a business, wanted to make sure it was recognized by the government, and wanted to keep it separate from your personal assets, then there are a few routes you could go – LLC, Sole Proprietary, or Corporation, to name a few. These all would be considered for-profit businesses because the revenue that the business produces goes straight into the pockets of the leaders of the organization. You can still do positive and meaningful work, but what you do with the profit changes. And, most importantly, any donations that a for-profit receives are not tax-exempt (more on this later).

Nonprofit

When you hear the term nonprofit, by definition it means that the leaders or board of directors of an organization do not directly receive the profit from the organization. Instead, the profit is meant to be invested back into the organization. Any company can be a nonprofit by this definition alone, but when you hear the term nonprofit, you more than likely are thinking about a 501(c)3. The 501(c)3 is a tax designation that means a charitable organization is 1) recognized under the IRS and 2) is determined as tax-exempt. It also means that the financial gifts donors give the organization are tax-exempt.

That is the 'what' behind a nonprofit, but why is it so important? In a world where there are tons of folks claiming to do something meaningful, a 501(c)3 status is one of the ways an organization can legitimize itself in the eyes of donors, members of the community, and other organizations. The IRS will not recognize just any organization as a 501(c)3 – as you will learn in this book. The application process is specific, intentionally intricate, and cryptic. Most philanthropies won't even consider giving to you unless you are a 501(c)3. While not all 501(c)3 organizations are great, it is the most common way for the public to know that the organization has gone through some type of vetting process to be a nonprofit.

So this goes back to the question – Does your idea need to become a nonprofit?

Typically, when I talk to a founder, they share a few reasons why the answer is **yes**:

- They are planning to receive a large donation and need to be a nonprofit to receive it,
- They partner with an organization in the public or social sector

(e.g. schools and churches) that only works with recognized 501(c)3s,

- There is no clear way for their organization to make money outside of donations. Being exempt allows for an easier path for them to receive donations,
- Or, sometimes, they just want to become a nonprofit! I have legit heard that as a reason, and guess what? That is fine too!

And just like there are a few reasons to have your organization become a nonprofit, a founder can also have their own reasons to take a business idea that can on the surface be a nonprofit and make it a for-profit. For example, I was working with a founder (let's call her Stephanie) who wanted to start a tutoring program in her hometown. We talked extensively for weeks about what nonprofits are, how they are governed, and fee-for-services vs fundraising. Ultimately, Stephanie decided to make the program a for-profit business strictly for the reason of not wanting her salary as the founder/CEO to be determined by a board of directors. Even though it was a group of folks she recruited, trusted, and knew would have the best interest of the tutoring program, Stephanie didn't want that level of authority given to anyone else besides her.

Here is a breakdown of some of the pros and cons of being a 501(c)3:

Pros	Cons
Tax exemption - you don't pay state or federal taxes, BUT you still need to file the appropriate paperwork for your state and Form 990 for the federal government on a regular basis.	Board members are volunteers and cannot get paid or be compensated for their time in the organization.

Pros	Cons
Donations are tax-exempt - anyone who gives you money can write that off for their taxes.	You have to follow a certain set of rules for-profits do not need to follow including lobbying, conflict of interest, etc.
There is a level of legitimacy that comes with being a recognized 501(c)3.	To become and maintain a 501(c)3, there is a lot of paperwork that needs to be filed and strict policies with submitting paperwork.

Still want to be a nonprofit? Great! Now your first step is to put together your board of directors.

WHAT IS MY VISION OF SOCIAL IMPACT?

IS A NONPROFIT RIGHT FOR ME?

Bring Together Your Board of Directors

Nonprofits are corporations. Corporations, by definition, are a group of individuals authorized to act as a single entity and are recognized as such by law. Not all for-profit businesses are corporations, but almost all nonprofits in the US are corporations in some way, shape, or form. This is to deter that a single person has complete power over an organization and also to deter conflict of interest (more on that later). To reiterate, a corporation is meant to be a legal way to divide power so one person cannot fully control how a business is run – and is something the government, and the IRS in particular, consider a requirement for an organization meant to be doing charitable/good work across the country.

So to have a nonprofit, you need to be a corporation. And to be a corporation, you need a board of directors.

A board of directors is the governing body of a company. What makes the difference between a for-profit board and a nonprofit board is that a for-profit board receives shares of profit from the company. Whatever revenue a company makes gets dispersed through shareholders – so the incentive for the board of directors is to have the company make A LOT of money so they can, in turn, make A LOT of money. A nonprofit board of directors is made up of volunteers who legally cannot receive profit or compensation from the nonprofit. Whatever revenue a nonprofit makes is reinvested into the organization. So the motivation of the board of directors is meant to be fully altruistic, wanting the best for the nonprofit and community the nonprofit impacts.

A board of directors is a very important part of any nonprofit, regardless of how big, small, young, or old the organization. They further legitimize themselves in the eyes of community leaders and donors and help guide the strategic direction of an organization. The nonprofit leader is managed by the board, their salary is set by the board, and the board hires them and has the power to fire them. Needless to say, picking the board for your organization is pretty important.

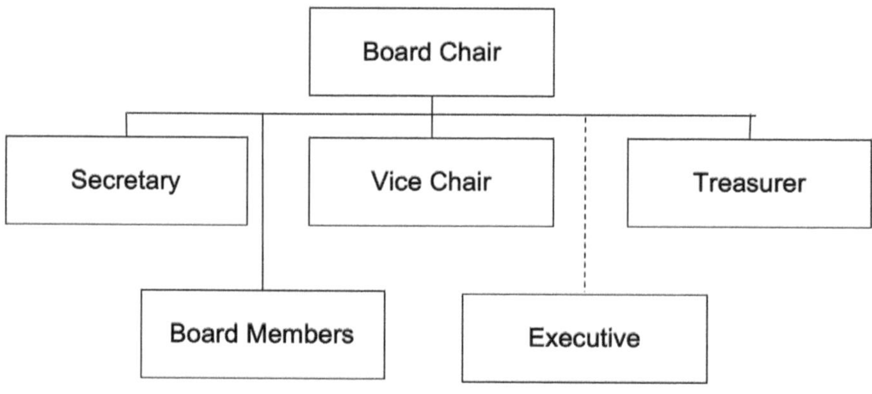

Putting together your Founding Board

When it comes to your founding board, the key is capacity-building. Think less about the title and funding capability someone has (that comes later) and more about what they can do to keep the ship afloat. Make sure you find ready-to-work, committed leaders who can help do the things you need to make your organization flourish and grow.

Remember Margaret Mead's famous quote: "Never doubt that a small group of thoughtful, committed citizens can change the world; indeed, it's the only thing that ever has."

A mental health nonprofit I consulted for early on had a board of three people, including the Executive Director. No one on the board was wealthy by any means, but they were all passionate about the work and believed in the leadership of the Executive Director. They spent 15 hours a week volunteering for the nonprofit by making phone calls, pitching the organization to funders and friends, and leading volunteers through activities. They were INVESTED and didn't receive a penny from the organization. Fast forward five years, the nonprofit is renowned for the work they have done in the mental health awareness space and has major corporate funders on its board. They would not have reached the levels they have if it wasn't for the committed group of board members they started with.

Here are a few things to keep in mind:

- Recruit at least 3-5 people committed to seeing the Corporation succeed. Different states have different requirements with the minimum number of board members you need. The majority require a minimum of three directors.
- They don't need to have fancy titles or big pockets. You may look for specific characteristics for board members once your organization is established, but for your founding board, the most important thing is commitment and work ethic.
- They must be able to hold the nonprofit leader accountable to see the organization flourish and thrive. More than likely, they will be recruited to be on the board by the Executive Director/CEO/Founder and will probably have a strong connection to them. That is fine, as long as they are the type of friend who is willing to tell the hard truth to the leader. The

Board of Directors needs to care about the success of the organization before anything else.

- They should understand that they will be volunteering their time, talent, and treasure. Essentially, they will be considered 'part-time employees' of the Corporation.
- They should commit to the role for at least two (2) years or until the Corporation is established enough to transition into a more mature/traditional board. Once the organization is more established and has consistent funding and staffing, then recruit specialists on the board who are there to help you with specific areas of the organization.

I'm often asked by clients what the makeup of a typical board should be for a nonprofit organization. My #1 answer is everything I said above, but for those who feel like they are ready for a more mature board of directors makeup, then consider:

- Founder - Champion of the mission and vision of the organization
- Philanthropist - Able to provide a substantial financial contribution to the organization and connect their network of wealthy individuals to support the organization as well
- Stakeholders of the organization - For example, if you provide scholarships to a school, either a student or staff member of the school could be on your board to help inform the experience of those who receive the organization's support
- Lawyer - Support with the legalese of business/nonprofit management. Usually plays the role of Secretary
- Accountant - Support with the financial monitoring of the business. Usually plays the role of Treasurer

Board Chair

If the Executive Director/CEO is the biggest cheerleader for the organization, the Board Chair is a close number 2.

The Board Chair is the organization's super-volunteer, sometimes serving as the de facto leader. Outside of leading the board of directors, the Board Chair supports, advises, and guides the Executive Director/CEO to successfully run the organization. Voting on the Board Chair is one of the most important decisions a board can make, especially on the founding Board Chair. They have to be a go-getter and make the organization a top priority for their time as the Chair.

A founder I worked with who spent the majority of her career in nonprofits (will call her Tiffany) took over a year to decide on her founding Board Chair. While Tiffany had a slew of volunteers she could count on to be on the board, she had seen too many instances where the chair didn't hold other board members accountable to play their part or where they micromanaged the Executive Director/CEO. Tiffany had seen, firsthand in organizations she worked in, a Board Chair manipulate the work of a founder/CEO and eventually remove them from their own organization. That is an outlier situation, but it was enough to leave an impact on this particular founder. After the year, Tiffany finally recruited a Board Chair who aligned with her morals, values, and vision for the nonprofit. Together, they established the culture for both the board of directors and the organization. The organization has had a thriving board ever since – even when the original Board Chair's term ended.

I cannot emphasize sufficiently the importance of this role. While a good Executive Director/CEO can make or break an organization, a good Board Chair can make or break an Executive Director/CEO. The Board Chair is the leader of the group who serves as the boss of the Executive Director/CEO and the person who will make sure they do everything they say they will do. Choose wisely.

How to Remove a Board Member

While I hope most of you reading this section believe you will never want to remove members of your board, I know and have consulted with enough leaders to know several folks are chomping at the bit for this section. Boards, for a lot of great things they can do for an organization, can cause a lot of pain for the Executive Director/CEO and the organization as a whole. Some have lied, caused the organization to lose money, micromanaged, been condescending to staff, and more. As a new nonprofit leader, you have to ask yourself, "Is this the right decision?" Board members are (technically) some of your organization's most dedicated and valuable volunteers. It is a big deal for someone to say 'yes' to being a board member, and it can be equally as big to be asked to no longer be in that role.

If, after dotting every "i" and crossing every "t," it still makes sense for this board member to no longer be on the board, then, in partnership with the Board Chair, a conversation with the board member should commence, specifically outlining the expectations of a board member and how this person isn't meeting those requirements. If this is the first conversation, then you should give the board member an opportunity to improve. If this isn't, then this is less of a conversation and more of an explanation of why the steps to have the board member removed are taking place. Make sure to review and follow the parameters listed in the bylaws to a tee.

If this conversation is for the Board Chair, then take the same steps as above, but input a strong, dedicated board member in place of the Board Chair.

Removing an underperforming, toxic, and/or inactive board member from your board can lead to very positive effects on a board – especially a small board. Board members have different reasons for joining a board – but one of the biggest is that it is a way to rub shoulders with other sector leaders who want to spend their time doing something positive. Having someone not uphold the expectations of the board can put a damper on the board experience for others. The inverse has a transformative effect as well.

WHO IN YOUR NETWORK DO YOU WANT TO BE ON YOUR BOARD?

WHAT KIND OF CULTURE DO YOU WANT TO SET FOR THE BOARD?

Create Bylaws

A nonprofit's bylaws, to say it simply, is the Constitution for an organization. It contains the majority of the rules and regulations that the board and leaders of the organization must follow. Why is it so important? Well, nonprofits are usually volunteer-led, so to make sure that the organization has consistency and efficiency in a fluid environment, bylaws are the constant that binds the organization together and guides the work of the board and staff. I often call it the Bible of the organization.

There are a couple of key items that every nonprofit bylaw should have. If you ever were to work with me, I would require that you have all of these sections included, or I wouldn't sign off on the bylaws. This is not because they are required, but to save you time because I can imagine you would come back to me in five years, expressing that there is a concern with your organization and you want a policy around it like something I originally mentioned. Trust me, you'll need it.

Sections in bylaws are typically called 'Articles.' Below are articles I suggest a nonprofit's bylaws should have:

Name -

Here you state the Legal and Doing Business As (DBA) Name of the organization

- Example - *The name of the corporation shall be ____________*

Purpose -

You can describe the mission and vision here if you like, but the most important thing in this section is to define that the organization is a 501(c)3.

- Example - *The Business is organized exclusively for purposes subsequent to section 501(c)(3) of the Internal Revenue Code.*

Membership -

Most new organizations are not membership organizations, so you would put 'no members' here. If you are a membership organization, like the YMCA/YWCA, etc., then you would define the components of being a member of your organization.

- Example - *In order to qualify for membership, a member shall be ____________. A member may be elected or appointed to membership by the Board. Members may have such other qualifications as the Board may prescribe by amendment to these Bylaws.*

Board of Directors -

Here you describe the roles and responsibilities of the board. You list how they vote, how meetings are structured, how someone is added to the board, what happens if someone is taken off the board, tenure, committees, officers, and more! Do not be surprised by the length of this section. Besides conflict of interest, this section should be the largest part of your bylaws. You list the key areas of who your board is and how they work with each other. When all else fails, the board will look at this document to move forward with a decision.

I recommend the following sub-articles:

- Powers
  - Example - *The Board of Directors shall have control of and be responsible for the management of the affairs and property of the Corporation.*
- Composition
  - Example - *The number of Directors shall be fixed from time to time by the Directors.*
- Tenure and Requirements
  - Example - *All Directors will be elected to serve three-year terms; provided, however, that the term may be extended until a successor has been elected. Directors may serve a maximum of two, three-year terms in succession, plus time served to fill a vacancy or a term of fewer than three years.*
- Meetings
  - Example - *An annual meeting of the Board of Directors shall be held at a time and day in the month designated by the Executive Committee of the Board of Directors.*
- Removal
  - Example - *A Director shall be subject to removal, with or without cause, at a meeting called for that purpose, by a majority vote of the Directors if in their judgment the best interest of the Corporation would be served thereby.*

Officers -

This section describes the roles and responsibilities of the officers of the board of directors. I recommend each board has three roles:

- Board Chair - Leads board meetings, serves as counsel to the

Executive Director/CEO, and holds the board accountable to do all the duties that are within the bylaws

- Secretary - Typically takes notes in board meetings, shares to-dos with board members, and updates the board on their duties between meetings
- Treasurer - oversees and keeps the Board informed of the financial condition of the organization. This includes reviewing financial audits, prepping the annual budget, etc.

Another role I typically have is the Vice Chair. The Vice Chair, like most other Vice roles, serves as the proxy/backup Board Chair. I often advise Board Chairs to treat the Vice as 'Board Chairs in training' and share part of the responsibility of the role with them.

These officers make up the Executive Committee. The Executive Committee members are the leaders of the Board and typically handle major decision items that they then present to the board for a vote.

Corporate Staff -

The day-to-day leader of your nonprofit organization is typically called your Executive Director or Chief Executive Officer (CEO). This section describes how the leader is hired and managed by the board and what steps to take to remove the leader.

This section is usually scary for a lot of nonprofit founders. The number one request I get from founders around their bylaws is for me to remove this section. The reason I don't is that this would make the organization no longer a corporation by definition because there would be no way to check the power of a single person. Philanthropic foundations typically avoid supporting organizations that do not have a clear system of checks and balances. So what can you do? The first thing I tell clients is to make sure they do a great job establishing the culture of their boards and recruiting strong board members. My second suggestion is for them to include language in the bylaws that gives special privileges to the founder/ founders including no board terms. Again, some philanthropic organizations frown on parameters like that and may not fund you unless those parts of your bylaws change.

- Example - *The Board of Directors shall hire an Chief Executive Officer/Executive Director who shall serve at the will of the Board. The Chief Executive Officer/Executive Director shall have immediate and overall supervision of the operations of the Corporation, and shall direct the day-to-day business of the Corporation, maintain the properties of the Corporation, hire, discharge, and determine the salaries and other compensation of all staff members under the Chief Executive Officer/Executive Director's supervision, and perform such additional duties as may be directed by the Executive Committee or the Board of Directors. No officer, Executive Committee member, or member of the Board of Directors may individually instruct the Chief Executive Officer/Executive Director or any other employee. The Chief Executive Officer/Executive Director shall make such reports at the Board and Executive Committee meetings as shall be required by the Board Chair or the Board. The Chief Executive Officer/Executive Director shall be an ad-hoc member of all committees.*

Amendments -

As your organization grows, there will be amendments that the board will need to make from time to time. It's not a question of IF, but WHEN. Almost every organization I've worked with needed to adjust their bylaws within the first five years of their existence – even bylaws that I helped personally create with the founders. It's inevitable. Below is a suggestion for how to word information about amending your bylaws

- Example - The Board of Directors may amend these Bylaws by majority vote at any regular or special meeting. Notice setting forth the proposed amendment or summary of the changes to be effected thereby shall be given to each director within the time and the manner provided for the giving of notice of meetings of directors.

Dissolution -

Simply put, your organization may not exist forever. Most funders want your bylaws to include how you will approach dissolution, a.k.a. dissolve your organization, and allocate its resources. There are a few ways you can word it, and I've included a standard one here:

Upon dissolution of the Corporation, the Board of Directors shall:

- Pay or make provision for the payment of all of the Corporation's liabilities;
- Return, transfer, or convey (or make provision therefor) all assets held by the Corporation upon condition requiring such return, transfer, or conveyance in the event of dissolution of the Corporation; and
- Distribute any remaining assets and property of the Corporation to such organization or organizations organized and operated exclusively for charitable or educational purposes as shall at the time qualify as an exempt organization under section 501(c)(3) of the Code as the Board shall determine.

There are several other items you can cover in your bylaws. A few popular items include indemnification, rules around taking out loans, and conflict of interest. The next section covers conflict of interest, so we won't touch upon it here.

WHAT CONCERNS DO YOU HAVE ABOUT ESTABLISHING BYLAWS?

HOW WILL YOU MAKE SURE YOUR BYLAWS ARE SET UP FOR THE BEST INTEREST OF YOUR ORGANIZATION?

Understanding Conflict of Interest

Speaking of checks and balances, this section is the area the IRS cares about immensely.

Every organization should have a conflict of interest policy. In fact, most philanthropic foundations require that an organization have a conflict of interest policy. What is a conflict of interest policy? In the simplest of terms, it ensures stakeholders in the business (board members, funders, staff members, etc) cannot directly benefit or influence benefits based on the organization's actions and decisions. For example, if a board member owns a restaurant, and the organization is looking for a place to hold a dinner event, a conflict of interest policy should make sure that several restaurants are presented as options to choose from (not just the board member's), and that board member doesn't vote on that particular decision since they could receive a financial benefit if the organization pays to use their restaurant.

Within your bylaws, you should state what the purpose of a conflict of interest policy is:

- Example - *The purpose of the conflict of interest policy is to protect this organization's interest when it is contemplating entering into a transaction that might benefit the private interest of a member of the board of directors of the Corporation.*

You'll then want to define who is capable of committing a conflict of interest to the organization:

- Example - *Any director, principal officer, or member of a committee with governing board delegated powers can commit a conflict of interest. (Oftentimes in bylaws they are listed as an Interested Person). A financial interest is not necessarily a conflict of interest. A person who has a financial interest may have a conflict of interest only if the Board or Executive Committee decides that a conflict of interest exists.*

Because of the sensitivity of this matter, you want to be exceptionally clear on the process the board should follow if there is a case of conflict of interest because it will need to be followed to the tee. They will dissect and analyze every step if it ever needs to be followed. Within the procedures, you should have these three terms:

- Duty to Disclose - In connection with any actual or possible conflict of interest, a director must disclose the existence of the financial interest and be allowed to disclose all material facts to the Board or Executive Committee.
- Recusal of Self - Any director may recuse themselves at any time from involvement in any decision or discussion in which the director believes he or she has or may have a conflict of interest, without going through the process for determining whether a conflict of interest exists.
- Determining Whether a Conflict of Interest Exists - After disclosure of the financial interest and all material facts, and after any discussion with the board member, they shall leave the Board or Executive Committee meeting while the determination of a conflict of interest is discussed and voted upon. The remaining Board or Executive Committee

members shall decide if a conflict of interest exists and what the appropriate repercussions should be.

State the procedures for addressing the Conflict of Interest. It's important for the policy to list very clear steps for the Board to follow when facing a potential conflict of interest. This will guide everyone and save concern, as this may be a sensitive topic for some. I have been called in as an outside advisor a few times to help facilitate Board Officers on how to conduct a process. The first question I ask is, "What does the policy say?" Usually, they are cryptic and poorly written – let alone if they exist at all. That is not ideal and can cause confusion and frustration for all parties – putting the organization at further risk. Take your time and be sure it makes sense to you and your board. I have an outline below that can help guide you in making your own policy:

- An interested person may make a presentation at the Board or Executive Committee meeting, but after the presentation, he/she shall leave the meeting during the discussion of, and the vote on, the transaction or arrangement involving the possible conflict of interest.
- The chairperson of the Board or Executive Committee shall, if appropriate, appoint a disinterested person or committee to investigate alternatives to the proposed transaction or arrangement.
- After exercising due diligence, the Board or Executive Committee shall determine whether the Corporation can obtain with reasonable efforts a more advantageous transaction or arrangement from a person or entity that would not give rise to a conflict of interest.
- If a more advantageous transaction or arrangement is not reasonably possible under circumstances not producing a conflict of interest, the Board or Executive Committee shall determine by a majority vote of the disinterested directors

whether the transaction or arrangement is in the Corporation's best interest, for its own benefit, and whether it is fair and reasonable. In conformity with the above determination, it shall make its decision as to whether to enter into the transaction or arrangement.

You'll also want to make it clear what the options are if someone were to be found having a conflict of interest. Remember, this is a BIG deal to the IRS – it's one of the BIG no-nos they have established for nonprofits, including lobbying/influencing policy and not filling out your annual 990. Here are some suggested steps:

- If the Board or Executive Committee has reasonable cause to believe a member has failed to disclose actual or possible conflicts of interest, it shall inform the member of the basis for such belief and allow the member to explain the alleged failure to disclose.
- If, after hearing the member's response and after making further investigation as warranted by the circumstances, the Board or Executive Committee determines the member has failed to disclose an actual or possible conflict of interest, it shall take appropriate disciplinary and corrective action.

For most board members, the concept of 'conflict of interest' makes sense, but every now and then you will need to educate them on the unique nature of how nonprofits operate as a business. Just because a specific purchase or partnership could be a good business move for a board member, that does not mean the organization should feel obligated to make such a move. Nonprofit organizations truly are meant to promote, support, and protect themselves.

While rare, I've worked with a few clients on moderating a conflict of interest case. The one that typically comes up is when a board member works in a similar industry as the organization for which they are on the board. For one organization, I shared that it appeared to be a conflict of interest and suggested the board officially go through a conflict of interest process. The board then voted that the board member could continue to operate as usual. Another example with another organization and the same setup: Board Member's job + conflict of interest + etc.; the process led to the board member being dismissed from the board. A key difference in the two cases was how trusting the board was of the person and if it was clear that the Board Member would fully prioritize the Organization over their personal interest. As I've shared earlier, nonprofit organizations are constantly trying to protect themselves – as they should. If the threat of a conflict of interest is there, the board has to do their due diligence – no one should take it personally.

WHAT ARE SOME POTENTIAL CONFLICTS OF INTEREST YOU FORESEE HAVING TO FACE?

HOW DO YOU WANT THE BOARD TO REACT WHEN THEY FACE CONFLICT OF INTEREST CASES?

The Basics of Fundraising

The first thing they tell you when studying social entrepreneurship is to make a plan for your organization to become sustainable. Sustainable means a lot of things in the nonprofit world, but for most people, like professors, they are referring to money. Money to a nonprofit is like gas to a car; the more of it you have, the farther you will go. How will your organization continue to consistently raise money?

So what should you do? Jim Collins says that the best companies find what they can do better than anyone else and capitalize on it. Nonprofits are very similar. Find out what you can contribute to the cause in such a unique and imperative way that the community is committed to seeing the success of your work.

Typically, very new nonprofits should look to be funded by philanthropists, community foundations, and grants that are specifically targeting the social cause you're addressing. Sponsors are important in nonprofit work, but just know that your first sponsor may take a long time to get on board as you continue to build your awareness, messaging, and your impact to showcase. Start-up nonprofits fundraise in similar ways to for-profit businesses with a few key differences:

Differences	Nonprofit	For-Profit (LLC, Corp, Sole Proprietorships)
Early-Stage Expectations (Friends and Family Round)	$1M (realistically 2 years of operating funds)	$1M
Venture Funders	Venture Philanthropist* (ex. New Profit,)	Venture Capitalist Firms (ex. Andreessen Horowitz)
Fundraising Materials	Pitch Deck (5-10 slides), Theory of Change, Scale and Growth Plan	Pitch Deck (10-20 slides), Financials, background of founders, demonstration of minimum viable product (MVP)
Stages of Start Up funding	Friends and Family, Seed Funding, Venture Philanthropy, General Fundraising Campaigns	Seed Stage (Friends and Family, Accelerators, Angel); Early Stage (Venture Capitalist); Late Stage (Series A, Series B, Series C)
Key Difference	Organizations are expected to land major gifts from local and national foundations to supplement Venture Philanthropy	Funding is meant to enhance MVPs, leading to additional sales and revenue for business

*Venture philanthropy is the nonprofit sector's version of venture capital, where funders provide funds, technical support, and more to support and spur social entrepreneurs to maximize and scale the impact of their ventures.

"So there are several kinds of funders, right? What should I know about them?" I'm glad you asked. Yes, there are some standard approaches for different funding groups. Following is a breakdown of each group:

Individuals & Corporations

When nonprofits receive donations from individuals, they are typically what the sector calls High Net-Worth Individuals (HNWI) – these are individuals who are able to make significant financial gifts (four figures or more) on an annual basis.

Corporations are for-profit businesses that have enough revenue so they can provide grants and funding to causes that align with their social impact/corporate social responsibility strategy. For example, Banks typically fund financial literacy and workforce development nonprofit organizations.

While both these groups are different, how you approach and engage with them should be the same:

- See who else they fund and whether there are similarities between the causes they fund and your organization
- Get connected with them through networking or cold outreach to see if they would be open to learning more about your organization
- Be clear about the needs you have and the plan for the future and see if they are willing to invest in the organization

This is, of course, easier said than done. While HNWI and corporations have the incentive to donate their funds to tax-exempt organizations and support causes that they care about, there are A LOT of organizations and causes out there, and they all are asking for money.

Foundations & Government

Foundations is a broad term that includes community foundations, family foundations, foundations that fund specific causes, and more. The thing they all have in common is they provide grants (funds awarded to organizations) to nonprofit organizations – so there is no need to dance around the fact that you are talking to them about how you can get money for your nonprofit.

Local and federal governments provide grants to nonprofit organizations to supplement the work that governments care about but don't have the day-to-day staff to operate. For example, if a local government cares about decreasing hunger, they may allocate millions of dollars in their annual budget to give grants to food banks and other social services in the local area.

While both groups are busy, they approach how they determine who they fund in similar ways. Because it is clear that they give money to nonprofits, you can imagine they receive TONS of applications and are looking for reasons to disqualify organizations – including making their application and reporting processes complex. Keep these things in mind:

- Make sure your organization aligns with what the foundation is looking to fund
- Provide ALL required documents, and fit EVERY required prerequisite (they won't even look at you if you don't)
- Be realistic and specific with what the organization will do with the awarded funds
- Try to meet with any Program Officer to share who you are and what you do
- Attend any grant-writing service/workshop the foundation holds

Events

Maybe you need to find alternative ways to raise money, or you need to do something to attract folks to come together to support your organization. What better way than to throw a fundraising event? Galas, luncheons with keynote speakers, silent auctions, and more are some ways you can throw a fun and engaging event that can attract and cultivate current and potential donors. You can raise money via ticket sales as well as through call-to-actions/ donation appeals during the event.

- Consider whether the event is for exposure (breaking even) or fundraising (making a profit)
- Don't overlook the cost of labor/time, regarding the cost benefit of the event
- Plan for solid advertising and recruitment strategies to meet your attendance goals
- Lastly, don't put all your hopes in your event to meet your fundraising goal IF this is new for you and your organization. It can potentially get to that point, but you may need to do this a few times before you can sense how successful a fundraiser can be for your organization.

Earned Revenue

If your organization can be paid by providing a service, fee-for-service, training others, selling a product, etc., that is a form of earned revenue. It is a popular and favorable option for nonprofits that avoids the hectic process of fundraising from donors. While it is favorable, not all nonprofits are able to receive earned revenue based on their programming – but if you are able to, you should do that. I've worked with an organization that's trainings earn close to 85% of their annual budget - the rest is made up by donations. The CEO spends the majority of his time landing training deals vs the majority of a nonprofit leader's job is to fundraise.

- Make sure that earned revenue programming aligns with the mission of the organization.
- Don't chase the dollar with a mindset of profit over authentic mission execution – you'll be better served running a for-profit business than a nonprofit.

Fundraising Materials

There are a few things every organization should have as they start to talk to funders and apply for funding. Here is a list of a few common materials:

- Pitch Deck - a brief presentation that provides an overview of your business plan, target stakeholders, services, and growth plans. The goal of a pitch deck is to communicate the value proposition of your organization clearly and concisely, convincing the audience to support your venture. The pitch deck should be visually appealing, clear, and to the point, aiming to capture the interest of your audience and generate further discussion.
- Theory of Change - a document that outlines a comprehensive description and illustration of how and why your organization will make the expected change in your impact area. The document often includes a visual representation, such as a flowchart or logic model, to illustrate the connections between activities, outputs, outcomes, and impact.
- Scale and Growth Plan - The scale and growth plan serves as a roadmap, guiding the organization through the steps necessary to achieve its growth objectives while ensuring that resources are used effectively and efficiently. The plans outline strategies and actions an organization will take to expand its operations and increase its impact or revenue, giving confidence to funders on the direction the organization is going.

HOW ARE YOU PLANNING TO RAISE MONEY FOR YOUR ORGANIZATION?

WHAT KIND OF CULTURE DO YOU WANT TO SET FOR THE BOARD?

Filing Registration Forms

Before we talk about all the paperwork it takes to be a nonprofit, first, we should further explain what a 501(c)3 is.

The 501(c)3 designation means that a charitable organization is recognized under the IRS and is tax-exempt. It also means that financial gifts that donors give to the organization are also tax-exempt. That is the what, but why is it so important? In a world where everyone claims to be doing something good, a 501(c)3 status is one of the ways an organization can legitimize itself in the eyes of donors, members of the community, and other organizations. Most philanthropies won't even consider giving to you unless you're a 501(c)3. While not all 501(c)3 organizations are great, it is the most common way for the public to know that the organization has gone through some type of screening process.

Becoming a 501(c)3 is equal parts easy and complex. There are a few government forms (listed below) that you will need to fill out to be recognized. The forms, in themselves, are often where I find the biggest barriers to entrepreneurs pursuing the 501(c)3 designation. Imagine a form asking questions about how you will expect to fundraise three years in the future if you never worked at a nonprofit before. Imagine your state forms were rejected because you didn't include a very specific and particular phrase you had no idea had to be mentioned in each form. Then, when you search for the answer online, everyone provides miscellaneous, confusing, conflicting, and bad advice. This is the current reality for many states that don't make the 501(c)3 process easy.

The process is not meant to be easy. If you look at any corporate crime that has occurred in the United States in the past 40 years, a nonprofit is involved in some way, shape, or form in almost all cases. As long as nonprofits are able to be tax-exempt, there will always be a desire by others to leverage the law in mischievous ways. The IRS and local governments know this and are not in a rush to make the process any easier. And, while nonprofits' process and overall structure might be complex and structurally intolerable, the crux is to protect organizations from nefarious characters within the organizations.

Below are general forms a nonprofit will need to complete in order to become designated a 501(c)3.

Articles of Incorporation

After thinking about the idea of your organization, putting together a board, and establishing your bylaws, the next step is to become an officially recognized organization. To become recognized as a corporation, you will need to register with your state government. This is usually the Secretary of State's office – or whichever department in your state handles business administration. Most states have a standard form you can fill out that asks for standard information like mailing address, name of board members, etc. One specific item that states require is for you to identify your registered agent. A registered agent is an individual or a business entity designated to receive legal documents and official government communications on behalf of a company.

The most important thing about a registered agent is they must have a mailing address in the state where you're filing your articles of incorporation. Typically, I suggest the founder be the registered agent so they can get any mail from the state. What mail can you expect? It will be mostly just reminders to submit your annual filing fee with the state. When should someone besides the founder be the registered agent? The only reason I would make this suggestion is if you wanted your nonprofit organization based in a state you didn't live in – then I would make someone you trust your registered agent.

Employer Identification Number (EIN)

This is a unique, nine-digit number assigned by the Internal Revenue Service (IRS) to businesses operating in the United States for the purpose of identification. It is also known as a Federal Tax Identification Number and is used by businesses for various tax and legal purposes. You can obtain your EIN from the IRS website after you receive confirmation that your organization is a certified corporation by your state. This is a very important number that you will use forever. Once you receive your determination letter from the IRS, your EIN will be what you provide to donors so they can claim their tax exemptions from donating to your organization.

Form 1023

Form 1023 is an application used by organizations to apply for recognition of tax-exempt status under Section 501(c)(3) of the Internal Revenue Code. Once approved, the organization receives a determination letter from the IRS confirming its tax-exempt status. This status allows the organization to be exempt from federal income tax and enables donors to make tax-deductible contributions.

There are two types of Form 1023 – the normal 1023 and 1023EZ. The normal Form 1023 is for organizations that have or will have over $50,000 annual revenue in the next three years; have over $250,000 worth of assets; and/or for any church, school, or hospital looking for tax exemption status. Form 1023 is a very long form that asks for several documents including board approved budgets, bylaws, and more. It can take up to nine months for the IRS to review and approve organizations that file with Form 1023.

Almost everyone who is reviewing this book should be filling out a 1023EZ. It is a much shorter, easier application than the standard Form 1023 and takes up to 2-3 months to get approval. The 1023EZ is an electronic form you can access through www.pay.gov. Within the application, you will file:

Part 1

Name and contact information for the organization, as well as for the members of the organization's board.

Most states require 2-3 board members. The IRS follows whatever your State requires. A standard title for your board member is DIRECTOR.

Part 2

Organizational structure for most applications will be corporation since you filed articles of incorporation for your state. The other options, including TRUST, are for other types of nonprofits that wouldn't be what you're looking for.

You would fill out the rest of your corporation's information and check the boxes showing that your organization will follow the regulations the IRS has for tax-exempt organizations.

Part 3

The National Taxonomy of Exempt Entities (NTEE) code is a three-character classification system used by the IRS to categorize nonprofit organizations. It helps in identifying the primary purpose and activities of a nonprofit. Simply look at the categories of NTEE codes and pick the best fit for your organization.

You'll then pick the purpose of your organization's focus. Most organizations are charitable (assisting those in need) or educational (intended or serving to educate or enlighten).

You'll then see a series of checkboxes where you should pick the appropriate box for your organization. For the yes/no checkboxes, most organizations will pick 'no' for all of the boxes in this section. If you pick 'yes', you will more than likely need to fill another form out in the future.

Part 4

This section helps to determine if you will be a public charity or a private foundation. A public charity raises money from donations from the general public or foundations. A private foundation typically gets all of its funds generally from 1-2 sources (Example - The Wells Fargo Foundation is a private foundation that receives almost all of its money from Wells Fargo). Almost everyone reviewing this book will be a public charity and should pick one of the first three boxes and, specifically, one of the first two boxes.

- Box 1a is for most nonprofit organizations that have been described throughout the book.
- Box 2a is similar to most nonprofits but also includes member organizations, like the YMCA, that rely on membership dues to pay for programming, or organizations that receive a significant amount of their revenue from an endowment or other investments

Part 5

This should only be filled out if your tax exemption status has been revoked. Hopefully, this won't be you!

Part 6

Sign and pay the filing fee and you're done! This needs to be electronically signed by one of the board members.

Form 990

Wait, you mean to tell me tax-exempt organizations still have to file taxes? Well...yes and no. Form 990 (including the EZ and postcard) is an annual document you share with the IRS to create a sense of transparency and clarity with the finances and operations of the organization. Nonprofits disclose several things, including donations and the highest salaried staff members. In order to maintain your exempt status, the IRS requires that the Form 990 is filled out and turned in annually. If you do not turn in the Form 990 three years in a row, your tax-exempt status is automatically revoked. There are three different kinds of Form 990, depending on the size of your organization:

990-N	Gross receipts normally less than $50,000
990EZ	Gross receipts less than $200,000, and Total assets less than $500,000
Standard Form 990	Anything greater than the 990EZ

WHICH STATE WILL YOU BASE YOUR ORGANIZATION AND WHY?

WHAT INFORMATION DO YOU NEED TO COLLECT TO GET STARTED FILLING YOUR PAPERWORK?

Closing

The hardest part of starting a nonprofit isn't putting together a board, filling out Form 1023, or even drafting your bylaws. In all the years, with all the entrepreneurs I've worked with, I've seen that the hardest part of starting a nonprofit is taking the first step. Many dreams and ideas have stopped before they ever had a chance to become real. Something that is needed to start a nonprofit and an aspect we did not cover in this guide is your 'why.' The Purpose of your organization. The Mission. The Vision. The idea for change that has been echoing in your brain every day. I cannot tell you when the time is right to start a nonprofit. There are many personal and professional factors to consider when starting an endeavor like this. What I can tell you is that your idea, your vision, and your dream should have a chance to see the light of day. Talk to someone. Write a business plan. Write the first word in your bylaws. Draw the logo. Do something! Give it a chance to breathe. Do it for your dream. Do it for your idea. And do it for the lives that will benefit from your organization's work.

I look forward to seeing the impact you'll make in turning your vision into reality!

Notes

www.ingramcontent.com/pod-product-compliance
Ingram Content Group UK Ltd.
Pitfield, Milton Keynes, MK11 3LW, UK
UKHW041643190726
13854UKWH00006B/2660